Creative Crafts for Kids

Backyard CRAFTS

By Greta Speechley

Gareth Stevens
Publishing

Please visit our Web site www.garethstevens.com. For a free color catalog of all our high-quality books, call toll free 1-800-542-2595 or fax 1-877-542-2596.

Library of Congress Cataloging-in-Publication Data
Speechley, Greta, 1948-
      Backyard crafts / Greta Speechley.
         p. cm. — (Creative crafts for kids)
      Includes index.
      ISBN 978-1-4339-3546-6 (library binding) — ISBN 978-1-4339-3547-3 (pbk.)
      ISBN 978-1-4339-3548-0 (6-pack)
      1. Handicraft—Juvenile literature. I. Title.
TT157.S654 2010
745.5—dc22   2009041569

Published in 2010 by
Gareth Stevens Publishing
111 East 14th Street, Suite 349
New York, NY 10003

© 2010 The Brown Reference Group Ltd.

For Gareth Stevens Publishing:
Art Direction: Haley Harasymiw
Editorial Direction: Kerri O'Donnell

For The Brown Reference Group Ltd:
Editorial Director: Lindsey Lowe
Managing Editor: Tim Harris
Children's Publisher: Anne O'Daly
Design Manager: David Poole
Production Director: Alastair Gourlay

Picture Credits:
All photographs: Martin Norris
Front Cover: Shutterstock: Asia Villafranca and Martin Norris

Manufactured in the United States of America
1 2 3 4 5 6 7 8 9   12 11 10

CPSIA compliance information: Batch #BRW0102GS: For further information contact Gareth Stevens, New York, New York at 1-800-542-2595.

Contents

Introduction

Backyard Crafts is packed with fun things to make. Learn how to paint stones to create pebble pets, build a rocket from a plastic bottle, or make a pretty vase for flowers. Look out for materials to use, such as pine cones, shells, and pebbles, in your backyard or on a country walk.

Getting started

 Read the steps for the project first.

 Gather together all the items you need.

 Cover your work surface with newspaper.

 Wear an apron, or change into old clothes.

A message for adults

All the projects in *Backyard Crafts* have been designed for children to make, but occasionally they will need you to help. Some of the projects do require the use of sharp utensils, such as scissors or a skewer. Please read through the instructions before your child starts work.

Making patterns

This is how you make the patterns on pages 30 and 31: Trace the pattern onto tracing paper using a pencil. If you're using fabric, cut out the tracing paper shape, and pin it onto the fabric. Cut out the shape. To cut the pattern out of cardboard, turn the tracing over, and lay it onto the cardboard. Rub firmly over the pattern with a pencil. The shape will appear on the cardboard. Cut out the shape.

Making stencils

To make the stencils that appear on page 30, follow the instructions for making a pattern; but instead of cutting out the shape, push your scissor points into the middle of the design. (Ask an adult to help you.) Now, carefully cut around the inside of the pencil outline, leaving a "window" in the paper or cardboard. This is the stencil.

When you have finished

Wash paintbrushes, and put everything away.

Put pens, pencils, paints, and glue in an old box or ice-cream container.

Keep scissors and any other sharp items in a safe place.

Stick needles and pins into a pincushion or a piece of scrap cloth.

BE SAFE

Look out for the safety boxes. They will appear whenever you need to ask an adult for help.

Ask an adult to help you use sharp scissors.

Bobbing boat

A homemade boat is great fun to sail around a pond or swimming pool. This one is made out of an empty ice-cream tub, but you can use any light plastic container. Just make sure it hasn't got any holes in it!

YOU WILL NEED

plastic container	toothpicks
white and colored cardboard	paintbrush
	clear glue
ruler	felt-tip pens
cardboard tube	black thread
	cord
acrylic paints	pencil
white paper	scissors

1 To decorate the boat, glue a narrow strip of colored cardboard and a length of cord around the outside of the plastic container.

6

tab	side panel	☐ ☐ ☐	roof	☐ ☐ ☐	side panel	tab

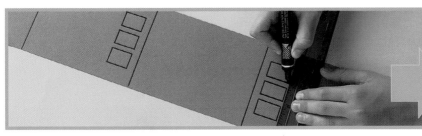

2 For the cabin, cut a strip of cardboard about 5in (13cm) wide and long enough to fit inside the boat when loosely formed into a cabin shape. Divide into three equal sections, as shown. Leave a tab of cardboard at each end of the strip. Draw windows on the side panels, and cut them out. Fold the cardboard along the lines, and glue the tabs to the bottom of the boat.

3 To make the funnel, cut the bottom off the cardboard tube at an angle. Paint the tube white, and decorate with stripes and a star. Glue the funnel to the cabin.

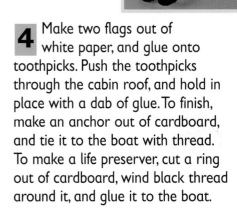

4 Make two flags out of white paper, and glue onto toothpicks. Push the toothpicks through the cabin roof, and hold in place with a dab of glue. To finish, make an anchor out of cardboard, and tie it to the boat with thread. To make a life preserver, cut a ring out of cardboard, wind black thread around it, and glue it to the boat.

Pebble pets

Take a look in your backyard for
some large, smooth stones to make
into pebble pets. You can make them
as cute or as scary as you like.

YOU WILL NEED

stones
acrylic paints
paintbrush
felt-tip pens
all-purpose
glue

seeds
acorn hats
wool
scrap paper
colored paper
scissors

CLEAR G

1 Paint the stones white and leave to dry. (The
white background makes the colors you paint
on later much brighter.)

8

2 Add a second coat of paint. We have used yellow for a flying pebble pet. Draw a design onto the stone using felt-tip pens.

3 Stick on buttons or acorn hats for eyes. Cut wings from scrap paper, or use sycamore seeds. Decorate with felt-tip pens. Glue in place.

4 To make a tail, cut a fringe into a square of colored paper. Fold in half, and glue to the back of the pebble.

5 To add a set of legs to a pebble monster, cut a zigzag edge into a length of paper, and stick the uncut edge to the pebble.

9

Vase of flowers

If you're eating outside on a hot, sunny day, a vase of colorful paper flowers will make a pretty table decoration. We have used tissue paper to cover the vase, but you could use strips of newspaper. Let the newspaper dry before you paint the vase.

YOU WILL NEED

tissue paper	plastic jar
paintbrush	string
PVA glue	acorns
garden stakes	buttons

1 To make the flowers, cut strips of tissue paper 12in x 4in (30cm x 10cm). Dilute the PVA glue with water, and cover the strips with glue. Fold the strips up lengthwise until they are about 1in (2.5cm) wide.

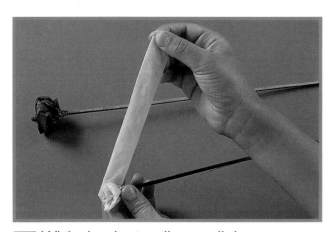

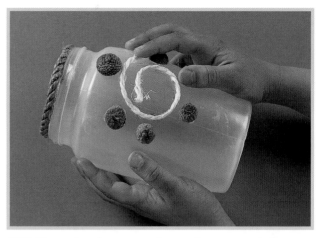

2 While the glue is still wet, roll the paper strips around one end of a garden stake. Scrunch up the paper to make a flower shape. Squeeze the bottom of the flower onto the stake. Hold in place for a minute or two. Let dry.

3 To make the vase, glue string around the top edge of the jar. Glue buttons, acorn hats, and a spiral of string to the front of the jar to make an interesting pattern.

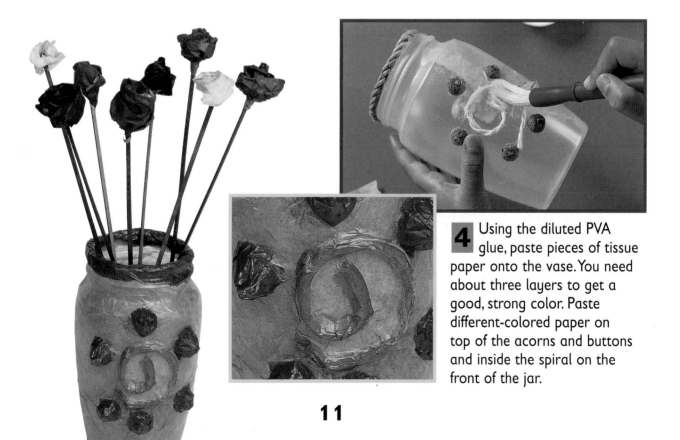

4 Using the diluted PVA glue, paste pieces of tissue paper onto the vase. You need about three layers to get a good, strong color. Paste different-colored paper on top of the acorns and buttons and inside the spiral on the front of the jar.

Birdseed cookies

The birds in your backyard will love these tasty cookies, especially in winter, when it is harder for them to find food. Try putting different seeds on each cookie to see which ones are eaten first!

YOU WILL NEED

cardboard	lard
scissors	knife
birdseed	ribbon
pencil	

Do not use margarine or fats other than lard to make the cookies. They have salt in them, which is bad for birds.

12

1 Draw some shapes onto strong cardboard, and cut them out. Make a hole in each shape. Ask an adult to help you do this.

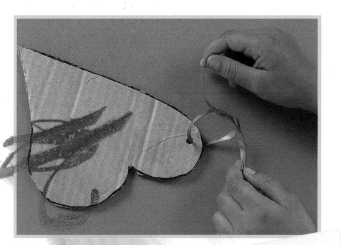

2 Thread a length of ribbon through the hole in each shape, and tie the ends together to make a hanging loop.

Ask an adult to help you make holes in the cardboard shapes.

3 Using a knife, spread softened lard all over the cardboard shapes.

4 Sprinkle birdseed onto the shapes, and press it lightly into the lard. Hang the finished cookies in your backyard.

13

Windmill

Put this bright, colorful
windmill in your
backyard, and watch
the sails spin around in
the breeze. When you
have made the
windmill, fill the bottle with sand
or water. That will keep it
from blowing over in
windy weather.

YOU WILL NEED

plastic
bottle

paper (for
stencil and
tassels)

pencil

tracing
paper

colored
cardboard

wooden
skewer

cork

barrel from
a felt-tip pen

large bead
or button

white and
blue acrylic
paints

PVA glue

glitter

sponge

scissors

paintbrush

1 Paint the bottle white.
When it is dry, sponge on
the pale-blue background. Trace
the star shapes on page 30, and
using a sponge, stencil dark-blue
stars on the bottle, as shown.
(See page 5 to find out how to
make a stencil.)

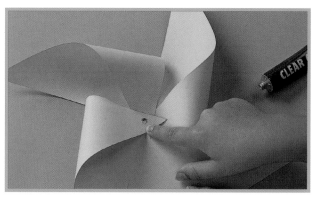

2 For the sails, cut a square 8in x 8in (20cm x 20cm) from colored cardboard. Mark the center point. Draw a line from each corner ending about 2in (5cm) from the center. Cut along the lines. Make a hole in each corner, as shown on the drawing above.

3 Make a hole in the center of the square. Fold over the points on the sails, as shown, and glue to the center, lining up the holes. Decorate the sails with paint and glitter, and add a tassel or a feather.

Ask an adult to help you cut the felt-tip pen barrel and the skewer.

4 Cut a section from the barrel of a felt-tip pen about 2½in (6cm) long. Ask an adult to do this for you. Push the barrel into the hole in the middle of the sails. Leave about ¾in (1.5cm) of the barrel sticking out at the front. Hold in place with a dab of glue.

5 Cut a piece of skewer about 3½in (9cm) long. Ask an adult to do this for you. Push the skewer through the barrel, and stick the pointed end into a cork.

6 Glue a button or a bead onto the front end of the skewer to keep the sails from coming off. To finish, stick the cork into the top of the bottle.

15

Flowerpot fairy

This cute flowerpot fairy will look very pretty hanging in your backyard. She's made from a selection of petals and leaves. We've used a plant called honesty to make the body. If you don't have this plant growing in your backyard, you could buy a packet of seeds and grow it for next year.

YOU WILL NEED

small plastic flowerpot	thin green pipe cleaner
cork (cut into two pieces)	polystyrene ball (from a craft shop)
leaves and flower petals	colored paper
acorns	large needle
thick green pipe cleaner	thread
2 shells	clear glue
	feathers

1 To make the body, glue honesty leaves and petals onto the flowerpot, overlapping them as you work.

16

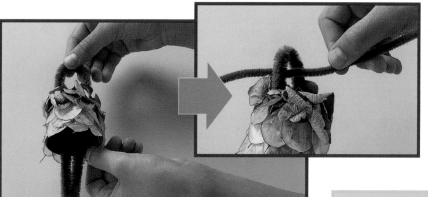

3 Tie one end of a long length of thread onto the loop made by the legs at the bottom of the flowerpot. Thread the other end into a needle. Push the needle through the polystyrene ball. Tie a loop in the thread so that you can hang up the fairy.

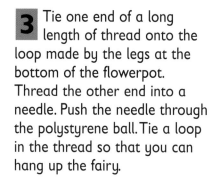

2 To make the legs, fold the thick pipe cleaner, and push the ends through the holes in the bottom of the flowerpot. To make the arms, slide the thin pipe cleaner through the loop made by the legs, as shown.

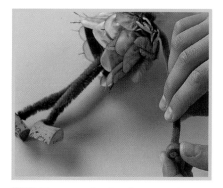

4 To attach the feet, push each pipe cleaner leg into a piece of cork. To attach the hands, push the arms into acorns.

5 Decorate the head with shells for eyes, strips of scrunched-up colored paper for hair, petals, and feathers.

Ask an adult to push the needle through the polystyrene ball. Ask an adult to cut the cork.

17

Catch a cone

This is a great game to play outdoors. Toss the pine cone into the air, and try to catch it in the cardboard cone. Make several cones in different colors, and invite your friends to come and play.

YOU WILL NEED

colored cardboard	glue
drawing pin	toothbrush
string	stapler
pencil	party streamer
scissors	paint
thin elastic	felt-tip pens
pine cone	

1 Tie one end of a piece of string to the drawing pin. Now tie a pencil to the string 7in (18cm) away from the drawing pin. Press the drawing pin into the corner of the piece of cardboard, as shown, and carefully draw a quarter-circle. Cut out the shape.

18

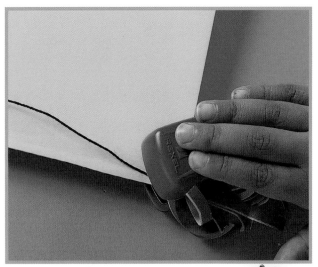

2 Draw a red wavy border around the top edge of the shape with a felt-tip pen. Paint or splatter a pattern on the cardboard using the toothbrush.

3 Staple a long length of elastic to the bottom point of the cardboard shape. Staple some short pieces of party streamer to the same place, as shown, to make a tassel.

4 Form the cardboard into a cone, and glue the edges together. (Make sure the elastic is on the inside of the cone and the tassel is on the outside.) Tie a pine cone to the end of the elastic.

Round houses

This village of round houses will make a fantastic decoration for your backyard in the summer. You can decorate the basic shape in any way you like. Try making temples or thatched huts, or even a city of skyscrapers.

Ask an adult to help you cut the plastic bottle.

1 Using scissors, cut the plastic bottle in half. Cut out a shape for the door. Ask an adult to help you with this step.

20

2 Stand the bottle on the cardboard, and draw around it. Cut out the cardboard circle inside the line. Cut a second cardboard circle slightly larger than the diameter of the bottle. Glue the circles together. Glue the bottle onto the smaller circle.

3 Glue short lengths of bamboo and twigs around the outside of the bottle to make the walls of the house.

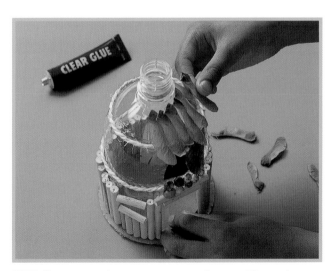

4 Continue decorating your house. To make separate stories, glue string around the bottle, and decorate each story with seeds and leaves. Leave spaces for windows. To finish, push a cork into the neck of the bottle, and add a little flag, or top with a pine cone.

Handy hint

Fresh seeds will shrink and fall off the bottle. Leave them to dry for a few days before you use them. To dry leaves, press them between two pieces of paper under a heavy book or in a flower press for a few days.

(Ask an adult before you take a book to use for pressing.)

Flyingfish kite

The design for this fabulous flyingfish comes from Japan, where kite-flying festivals are held every year. Attach a long length of thread to your fish so that you can fly it around your backyard.

YOU WILL NEED

colored tissue paper

tracing paper

felt-tip pens

glue stick

glitter pens

thin white cardboard

needle and thread

pencil

scissors

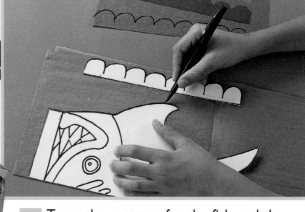

1 Trace the patterns for the fish and the scales on page 31. (Read the instructions on page 5 to find out how to do this.) Cut the patterns out of paper. Fold a piece of tissue paper in half, and place the fish pattern against the fold. Draw around the pattern, and cut out the fish. Cut out seven rows of scales from different colored tissue paper.

22

2 Open out the fish shape, and lay it back onto the pattern. Using a black felt-tip pen, trace the markings onto the fish. Trace one side first, then turn the pattern over, and trace the markings onto the other side of the fish.

3 Color in the mouth, eyes, and other markings using felt-tip pens. Stick on the scales starting at the tail, overlapping them as you work. Trim to fit the fish.

4 Using the black felt-tip pen, outline the fish scales. Dab dots of glitter onto the fish with a glitter pen.

5 Cut a strip of white cardboard the same length as the mouth and half the width. With the wrong side of the fish facing you, stick the cardboard to the bottom edge of the mouth, and fold over the tissue paper.

6 Put a thin layer of glue around the edge of the fish, and glue it together. To finish, thread a needle with thread, and sew through the top edge of the mouth. Knot the ends together. Leave one long length of thread to hang up the fish.

23

Ice catcher

When the sun shines on a cold and frosty day, this pretty ice catcher will shimmer and glisten in the trees. Make several ice catchers, and hang them in your backyard for Christmas.

YOU WILL NEED

round waterproof tin	a small stone
water	leaves, petals, grasses, and flowers
string	

1 Carefully fill the tin with about 1in (2.5cm) of water.

24

2 Tie a loop in one end of a length of string. Drop the other end into the water, and weigh it down with a small stone. This will keep the string in place.

3 Collect some pretty flowers, leaves, and grasses. Choose the ones you would like to use to make your ice catcher.

4 Arrange the leaves and petals in the water. Long grasses look pretty wound around the edge. Put the tin into a freezer. Once the ice catcher has frozen, you may need to dip the bottom of the tin into lukewarm water to release it. Ask an adult to help.

Ask an adult to help you remove the frozen ice catcher from the bottom of the tin.

25

Racing rocket

This colorful rocket has hooks on the top so that it can whiz along a length of string tied up in your backyard. If you put some water in the bottle, it will go even faster!

YOU WILL NEED

large plastic bottle	colored cardboard
2 cup hooks	scissors
2 corks	paper and pencil
skewer	tracing paper
sponge	PVA glue
felt-tip pens	acrylic paints
shiny paper	

1 Cut the bottom off the plastic bottle. Using a skewer, make two small holes in the side of the bottle about 7in (18cm) apart. Hold the corks inside the bottle over the holes. Screw the cup hooks through the bottle and into the corks. Ask an adult to help you with this step.

3 Draw three funny pictures small enough to fit in the windows of your rocket. Draw a circle around each picture, and cut out. Glue the circles inside the bottle in the windows.

2 To make the windows, cut three circles out of paper, and stick lightly to one side of the bottle. Using a sponge, dab paint all over the bottle. Paint a pattern on the cone, neck, and top of the bottle. Let dry. Peel off the paper circles.

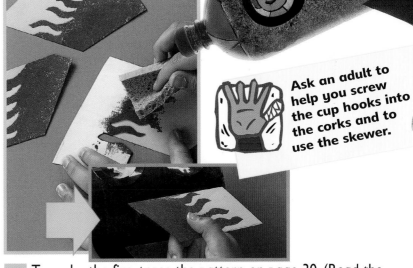

Ask an adult to help you screw the cup hooks into the corks and to use the skewer.

4 Cut three rings of shiny paper big enough to fit around the paper circles. Stick the rings to the outside of the bottle to make window frames.

5 To make the fins, trace the pattern on page 30. (Read the instructions on page 5 to find out how to do this.) Cut four fins from cardboard. Cut away the shaded part of the pattern, to leave the flames. Lay the pattern on each fin, and sponge on red paint, as shown. Fold back one long edge on each fin, and glue to the rocket.

Turtle mosaic

Made from pebbles, recycled glass, seeds, and shells, this stunning turtle mosaic would make a fabulous present. Follow the instructions shown here, or try creating your own design.

1 Trace the turtle on page 30. (Read the instructions on page 5 to find out how to do this.) Make sure that you have a tray or a lid that is big enough to hold your mosaic.

2 Arrange the seeds, recycled glass, shells, pebbles, and other materials onto your drawing.

3 When you are happy with your design, fill the tray with tile cement.

4 Now transfer the pebbles, seeds, and other materials onto the tray, copying the paper design carefully. Press each pebble and seed into the tile cement. When you have finished, leave the mosaic in a safe place to harden. You can spray your finished mosaic with varnish to make it shiny and weatherproof.

Patterns and stencils

Here are the patterns and stencils you will need to make some of the projects in this book. To find out how to make a pattern and a stencil, follow the instructions on page 5.

Windmill
page 14

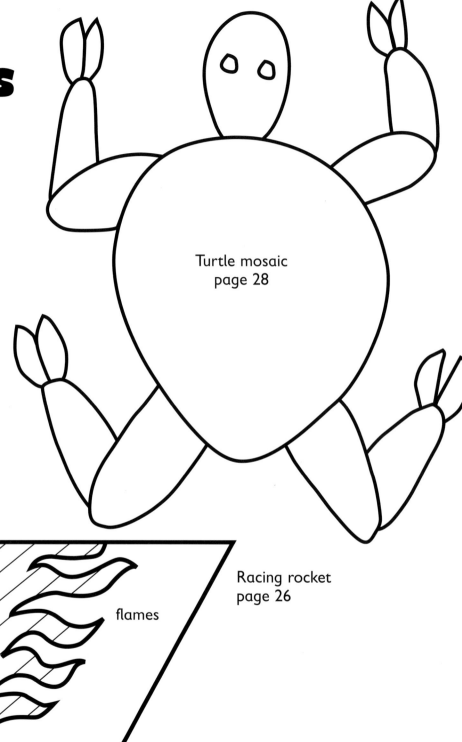

Turtle mosaic
page 28

Racing rocket
page 26

flames

rocket fin

Flyingfish kite
page 22

scales

Flyingfish body

31

Glossary

acrylic paint a paint, used especially for painting pictures, that is made with a manufactured acid

dilute to make something thinner or weaker by adding water or another liquid

fringe a decorative border consisting of short strands of thread or other material

life preserver a ring, belt, or jacket made of material that floats in water

mosaic a picture or design made of small pieces of colored glass or tile stuck to a surface

polystyrene a manufactured material, often in the form of rigid white foam

PVA glue one of the most common glues. "PVA" stands for polyvinyl acetate.

skewer a thin metal or wooden rod with a pointed end

stencil to apply a design to a surface using a pattern

tassel a bunch of loose threads tied together at one end that is used as decoration

varnish a substance that gives an object a protective gloss, or the act of applying this substance

Index